Sell on a Large Scale

Lucie Dupont

Lucie Dupont

Lucie Dupont

Copyright Page

Index

Understanding Scalability — 7
Global Market Research — 13
Strategic Planning for Global Expansion — 20
Cultural Aspects in Global Sales — 28
Digital Strategies for International Trade — 36
Logistics and International Supply Chain — 44
Legal and Regulatory Compliance in International Sales — 53
International Taxes and Tariffs — 61
Payment Methods and Currency Management in International Markets — 69
Contracts and Negotiation in International Sales — 77
Pricing Strategies for International Markets — 86
Customer Service and Support in the Global Market — 95
Building International Sales Teams — 103
Constant Innovation and Adaptation — 110

Lucie Dupont

Understanding Scalability

Scalability is a key concept when talking about expanding a business, and it refers to a company's ability to grow without losing efficiency or quality in its operations. Imagine your business is a small local store that sells products efficiently in your city. Now, if you wanted to open other stores in different cities or even in other countries, you would need to make sure that the business can continue to operate with the same level of quality and success. This is what it means to be scalable: the ability to grow while maintaining the same structure, or adjusting it, without the increase in size bringing with it a drop in performance.

For a business to be scalable, it must have systems and processes in place that allow for increased production, distribution, and sales without a proportional increase in costs or the time required to run the business. For example, if your business model requires a lot of personalized attention for each customer, it can be difficult to maintain that same quality of service when you have hundreds or thousands of additional customers in other markets. This is where tools and strategies to automate or simplify processes come into play, so that the business can grow without overwhelming the people who run it.

Scalability isn't just about doing more of what you're already doing, it's about doing it smarter. It's about finding ways to reach more people without having to spend a proportionally larger amount of time, money, and effort. To illustrate, let's think of a simple example: if you have a factory that produces shirts, and each shirt costs you ten dollars in materials and two hours of labor to make, if you wanted to produce twice as many shirts, would you need twice as much money and time? If you haven't set your business up for scaling, the answer may be yes. But if you've designed a system where producing in higher volume reduces the cost per unit, and at the same time you've found ways to automate some of the work, then you can double your output without doubling your costs or time invested. That's scalability.

Another key aspect of scalability is knowing when and how to expand your business. It's not just about having the ability to grow, but doing so at the right time. If you try to expand too quickly without having the necessary resources or infrastructure, you may risk making your business inefficient. Conversely, if you wait too long, you could miss out on valuable opportunities to grow in markets that might have been a perfect fit for your product or service. That's why it's important to understand your current capacity and carefully plan when you expand.

Technology plays a crucial role in the scalability of any business today. Digital tools allow companies to reach global audiences with relative ease. A website, an e-commerce platform, or even social media can be powerful instruments to scale your business without requiring a huge investment. However, while technology makes many things easier, it is also important to remember that behind every great scalable business there is a solid strategy. It is not just about selling more, but doing so in a way that each new sale is more profitable and more efficient than the last.

When talking about scalability, it is also essential to mention the team that makes this growth possible. Having a committed and well-organized team is key for a company to be able to expand successfully. As a business grows, the roles and responsibilities of the people within the company must also adapt. The same people who managed a small local business cannot be expected to handle an international operation in the same way without a proper structure. Therefore, part of being scalable involves having the right team and the necessary skills to manage growth.

Finally, it's important to remember that scalability isn't just a goal, but an ongoing process. It's not something you achieve overnight, nor is it something you can do once and forget about. Scaling a business involves constantly evaluating, adjusting, and improving systems and processes to ensure that as the company grows, efficiency isn't lost or costs are increased unnecessarily. Every new market, every new product, and every new customer represents an opportunity to scale efficiently, but they are also challenges that require planning and strategy.

In short, understanding scalability is critical for any entrepreneur who wants to expand their business into other countries or markets. It means creating a business model that can grow without losing its ability to generate profits efficiently. It means knowing when and how to expand, and having the right tools, technology, and team to do so. And above all, it means always being prepared to adjust and improve the processes that allow you to continue growing without losing quality along the way.

Lucie Dupont

Global Market Research

Global market research is the essential first step when thinking about expanding a business beyond national borders. Before entering a new market, it is crucial to understand the specific characteristics of local consumers, their needs, their behaviors, and the opportunities that the market can offer. This research will not only help you better understand the territory you want to reach, but it will also allow you to avoid costly mistakes by making strategic decisions based on solid data and not assumptions.

Getting started with good global market research is like mapping out the terrain before setting out on a journey. It's not just about knowing where you are and where you want to go, but also knowing the obstacles in your way and the best routes to overcome them. Every country has its own particularities, and what works in one market may not be effective in another. For example, a product that is popular in Europe might not be as popular in Asia due to cultural, economic or even climatic differences. Understanding these differences is key to adapting your offer and your sales strategy.

One of the first steps in global market research is gathering demographic data. This means gathering information about age, gender, income level, education, and other factors that help you define your potential customers in each country. If your product is primarily targeted at young, high-income adults, it's important to make sure that there are a significant number of people in your target market who fit that profile. Otherwise, you could be investing time and resources in a market that doesn't have enough demand for your product or service.

Another crucial part of research is understanding local consumer habits. What types of products do people buy? How often do they make those purchases? Do they prefer to shop in physical stores or online? What factors influence their purchasing decision, such as price, quality, or brand? These are critical questions that will help you fine-tune your approach. For example, in some countries, consumers may be extremely price-sensitive, meaning your pricing strategy will need to be highly competitive. In other markets, consumers may value quality or brand reputation more, which could allow you to sell products at higher prices if you can demonstrate superior value.

Competitor analysis is also a key component of global market research. You need to know who your competitors are in each market, what they offer, and how they are offering it. You may be up against local competitors who are already well-established and who better understand local consumer needs. Studying these competitors can give you a clear idea of what you need to do to differentiate yourself. You may find that you can compete on price, quality, innovation, or customer service, but you will need this information to make informed decisions.

In addition to studying your competition, it's also important to pay attention to market trends. Markets are constantly changing, and what's popular today may not be popular tomorrow. Trends can be technological, such as the rise of e-commerce in some regions, or cultural, such as the growing interest in sustainable or eco-friendly products in certain countries. Staying on top of these trends will allow you to stay ahead of market needs and adapt your offering before your competitors do.

Global market research isn't a one-time thing. Instead, it's an ongoing process. Markets evolve, and what was true when you entered a country might change over time. That's why it's critical to continue collecting data and monitoring the market environment to ensure your strategy remains relevant. This includes staying on top of economic, political, or social changes that may impact your sales. For example, an economic crisis in one country might cause consumers to cut back on spending, while new government regulation could impact how you can sell your product.

Sources of information for global market research can be varied. First, you can turn to existing studies conducted by consultancies or agencies specializing in market analysis. These agencies often offer detailed reports on consumer trends and behaviors in different countries. However, it is also valuable to conduct your own research, which is known as primary research. This can include surveys, interviews, or focus groups with local consumers. These tools allow you to gain direct insight into what people in the market you want to enter think and need.

Another useful tool for global market research is the use of technology. The Internet has made it easier than ever to research international markets from anywhere in the world. Social media, for example, allows you to observe how consumers interact with different brands and products, giving you insight into what they value. E-commerce platforms like Amazon can also give you data on what types of products sell best in certain regions. Additionally, web analytics tools like Google Trends can show you what searches are popular in different countries, giving you insight into emerging consumer needs.

Finally, it's important to remember that global market research isn't just an exercise in collecting data, but a way to prepare yourself to make smarter decisions. Every piece of information you gather should help you adjust your sales strategy, from the design of your product to the way you communicate with your customers. It's not just about launching a product on the market and hoping it's successful, but about tailoring your approach so that it truly resonates with the people you're targeting.

In short, global market research is the foundation of any successful international expansion. It is a process that allows you to thoroughly understand the markets you want to operate in, identify opportunities and challenges, and adjust your strategy to maximize your chances of success. By understanding your consumers, your competitors, and market trends, you will be better equipped to make informed decisions that will help you grow and prosper in international markets.

Lucie Dupont

Strategic Planning for Global Expansion

Strategic planning is the backbone of any successful global expansion. Before you set out to sell overseas, you need a well-structured plan to guide you through every step of the process. It's not just about deciding that you want to sell internationally, but about mapping out a clear path to achieve that goal, taking into account all the key aspects that will influence the success of your expansion. Without a solid plan, it's easy to get lost in the complexities of foreign markets and encounter unexpected obstacles.

The first thing you need to do in strategic planning for global expansion is to clearly define your goals. Why do you want to expand? What do you hope to achieve? These goals should be specific and measurable. For example, instead of simply saying you want to "increase your sales," you could set more concrete goals, such as "increase sales by 20% in the European market over the next two years." Setting clear goals will give you an accurate view of what you want to achieve and help you evaluate your progress as you go.

Once you have defined your objectives, the next step is to research and choose the markets you want to enter. Not every country will be suitable for your product or service, so it is essential to identify those that have the greatest potential. As we saw in the global market research, you need to take into account factors such as market size, consumer purchasing power, competition and barriers to entry. A common mistake is trying to enter too many markets at once. Instead, it is advisable to start with one or two key markets, where you have the greatest chance of success, and then expand gradually.

An important aspect of strategic planning is defining how you will adapt your product or service for new markets. What works in your home country may not be well received in other parts of the world. Consumer preferences vary greatly from country to country, so you will need to adjust certain aspects of your offering. This could include changes to product design, packaging, pricing, or even brand name. Adapting to cultural and local differences is crucial to making your business feel relevant in a foreign market. While it may seem tempting to try to keep your product exactly as it is, a small modification that reflects local expectations can make the difference between success and failure.

Another factor you need to consider in your plan is how you will handle the logistics of selling in other countries. This includes things like distribution, shipping, delivery times, and after-sales service. In some countries, you may need to set up local warehouses or distribution centers to get your products to consumers faster. Additionally, you will need to consider the costs associated with international transportation and potential import duties and fees. Having a clear logistics strategy is essential to ensure that you can meet your customers' expectations, no matter where they are in the world.

The next step in your strategic planning is to decide how you are going to enter those markets. There are several ways to do this, and choosing the best strategy will depend on your goals and resources. One option is to establish a physical presence in the country, such as opening a local office or store. This is a more expensive strategy, but may be necessary if you need to be close to your customers or if your product requires a high degree of personal interaction. Another option is to collaborate with local distributors or partners, who already have experience in the market and can help you navigate the complexities of operating in that country. You can also choose to sell online through global e-commerce platforms, which will allow you to reach a wider audience without the need for a physical infrastructure.

Marketing strategy is also a key part of your expansion plan. You need a way to get the word out about your product or service in the new market, and that requires an approach tailored to local consumer preferences and behaviors. Marketing strategies that work for you in your country may not be as effective elsewhere. For example, in some markets, social media ads can be very effective, while in others, traditional TV or radio advertising is still the best option. Additionally, the way you communicate with customers needs to take into account cultural sensitivities and linguistic nuances. It's critical that your message is clear and relevant to the audience you're targeting.

An often overlooked aspect of strategic planning for global expansion is human resource management. Expanding into new markets means managing teams in different locations, with different work schedules, languages, and cultures. You will need to develop a strategy for hiring and training local employees or assigning team members to new markets. It is critical that employees understand cultural differences and are prepared to work in an international environment. A well-trained and engaged team will be one of the keys to your successful expansion.

It's also important to plan how you're going to fund your expansion. Entering new markets requires investment, and it's critical that you have a solid financial plan to support your goals. This includes anticipating entry costs, such as marketing, operations, and logistics, as well as potential challenges that may arise along the way. You may not see an immediate return on your investment, so you should be prepared to endure a few months, or even years, before your expansion starts to generate significant profits. Having a financial cushion or access to adequate sources of funding can make all the difference in the sustainability of your global expansion.

Finally, a crucial part of strategic planning is establishing a system for monitoring and evaluating your results. It's not enough to simply implement the plan and hope for the best. You'll need to constantly monitor the progress of your expansion and adjust your strategy as needed. This means keeping an eye on sales, consumer response, local team performance, and changes in the market. Sometimes what seems like a great opportunity may not yield the expected results, and it's critical to be prepared to make tough decisions, such as pulling out of a market that isn't performing or redirecting resources to one that's showing greater potential.

In short, strategic planning for global expansion is a detailed process that requires attention to many factors. From setting clear goals to adapting your product and designing marketing strategies, each step must be carefully thought out and executed. In addition, it is essential to be prepared for the logistical, financial and operational challenges that will arise when selling in other countries.

With a well-structured plan, you will be able to minimize risks and maximize opportunities for your business to grow sustainably in the global market.

Lucie Dupont

Cultural Aspects in Global Sales

Cultural aspects are a fundamental piece of global sales. When expanding your business to other countries, it is essential to understand that you are not only moving into a new market, but also into a completely different cultural environment. What may be effective for selling in one country may not work in another, and the key to successful global expansion is knowing how to adapt to these cultural differences. Ignoring these factors can lead to misunderstandings, frustrations, and ultimately, lost sales. Therefore, knowing and respecting the customs, values, and norms of each culture will allow you to build stronger relationships and increase your chances of success.

The first thing to consider is how different cultures view business interactions. For example, in some cultures, such as the United States or Germany, negotiations tend to be direct and results-oriented. In these cultures, business is focused on efficiency, and customers value clear and prompt communication. In contrast, in countries such as Japan or China, the negotiation process tends to be slower, as personal relationships and trust are highly valued. In these cases, you may need to spend time building a strong relationship before the customer is willing to close a deal. Ignoring these differences can make international customers feel uncomfortable or even offended.

Language is another key factor in global sales. Although English is widely used in international business, not all markets are comfortable using it. Therefore, if you really want to connect with your customers, it is advisable to adapt your communication to their local language. This not only includes translating your website, marketing materials and contracts, but also taking into account the cultural nuances of the language. A literal translation is not always enough, as some expressions or terms may not have the same impact or meaning in other cultures. Investing in high-quality translations and adaptations can make a huge difference in the way your product is perceived.

Another important cultural aspect is the way roles and hierarchies are perceived in different parts of the world. In some countries, business decisions are made collaboratively and horizontally, where everyone in the organization has a say in the process. This is common in many Western cultures, where participation and consensus are valued. However, in other cultures, such as those in many parts of Asia and the Middle East, business structures tend to be more hierarchical. In these cases, only people in positions of authority are likely to have the ability to make important decisions, and it is critical that you identify who has the decision-making power within a company or institution. If you try to negotiate with the wrong person, you could waste valuable time or even ruin your opportunities.

The concept of time also varies greatly between cultures and can affect your overall sales. In some countries, such as the United States or Germany, punctuality and respect for deadlines are key. Arriving late to a meeting or failing to meet agreed-upon deadlines can be seen as unprofessional. On the other hand, in cultures such as those of many Latin American countries or Southern Europe, the concept of time is more flexible. Meetings may start later than planned, and deadlines may be seen more as guidelines than strict rules. If you don't understand these differences, you could frustrate yourself or your clients.

In addition to time perception, forms of greeting and physical contact also play a major role in global sales. In some countries, such as Japan, a formal greeting may involve a slight nod, while in Spanish-speaking countries, a firm handshake or even a hug is common if the relationship is closer. In other cultures, such as many Arab countries, a longer greeting is expected, with questions about family and personal life before discussing business. Ignoring these norms can make your customer feel uncomfortable or misunderstood. The key here is to be aware of social expectations and follow local customs to demonstrate respect and professionalism.

Communication style also varies considerably between cultures. In some countries, such as the United States or Germany, communication is often direct and to the point. People value directness and clarity, and do not tend to surround the subject with subtleties. However, in other countries, such as Japan, India, or many Middle Eastern countries, communication can be more indirect and diplomatic. In these cultures, business is conducted in a more reserved manner, and you are expected to read between the lines to understand what is really being said. In these environments, it is important to be patient and not push too hard for quick or direct answers, as this can be seen as tactless.

In addition to behaviors and language, it is crucial to understand the values and beliefs that motivate consumers in different parts of the world. For example, in many countries in Europe and North America, consumers may be very focused on price and quality, while in markets such as Japan, brand loyalty and company reputation are extremely important. In some countries, consumers value products that reflect innovation and modernity, while in others, traditional and artisanal products are in high demand. Knowing these cultural preferences will allow you to tailor your product and marketing strategy to better resonate with your customers.

It's also important to consider holidays and public holidays in different countries. For example, trying to close a big deal during Chinese New Year, when many businesses are closed, would be a strategic mistake. Similarly, in Muslim countries, the month of Ramadan can affect work schedules and consumer dynamics. Knowing these details and planning around them will help you avoid inconveniences and show respect for local traditions.

Customer service culture also varies considerably between countries. In some cultures, customers expect extremely attentive and personalized service, while in others, they prefer a more discreet and less intrusive interaction. In countries like the United States, consumers value speed and efficiency, while in Japan, quality and detail in service are paramount. Adapting the way you offer customer service to local expectations will help you build stronger relationships and generate greater customer satisfaction.

In short, cultural aspects of global sales are critical to understanding how to interact with customers and business partners in other countries. From differences in communication to expectations about customer service, each culture has its own norms, customs, and values that influence the success of a business transaction. By taking the time to learn and adapt to these differences, you'll be in a better position to connect with your international customers, earn their trust, and increase your sales globally.

Lucie Dupont

Digital Strategies for International Trade

In today's world, digital strategies are an indispensable tool for any company that wants to succeed in international trade. The Internet and digital technologies have broken down many of the traditional barriers that existed between countries, allowing companies to reach customers around the world without needing to have a physical presence in each market. This has opened up a world of opportunities, but it has also created new challenges that require a strategic approach in order to make the most of the digital resources available. Implementing effective digital strategies is key to positioning yourself correctly in international markets and growing your business on a global scale.

One of the first things to consider in a digital strategy for international trade is having a strong online presence. Your website will, in many cases, be the first point of contact between your company and international customers, so it's essential that it's well designed, easy to navigate and optimised for all devices. In addition, it's crucial that your website is available in multiple languages, depending on the markets you're targeting. It's not just about translating content, but about making sure that the version of your website in each language is culturally adapted to local expectations and preferences. A customer in Japan will have different expectations than a customer in Germany, and it's essential that your website reflects these differences to create a positive user experience.

In addition to your website, social media plays a key role in any digital strategy for international trade. Social media allows you to interact directly with your customers in real time, create a community around your brand, and build trust in new markets. However, just like with your website, it's important to tailor your social media approach to each market. The most popular platforms vary by region. For example, while Facebook is very popular in many Western countries, in China, the most widely used platform is WeChat, and in Russia, VKontakte. It's essential to identify which platforms your potential customers use the most in each country and adjust your content and advertising strategy accordingly.

Content marketing is also a key digital strategy for international trade. Publishing relevant and valuable content not only improves your visibility in search engines, but also helps you build a relationship of trust with your customers. Creating a blog in multiple languages, producing explanatory videos, or publishing guides that answer your customers' most common questions in each market can position you as an authority in your industry and attract new buyers. As with other aspects of digital marketing, it's important to customize content for each market. Content preferences vary greatly from country to country; while in some places consumers prefer to read long-form articles, in others they prefer to consume more visual content, such as videos or infographics.

One of the most powerful tools in any international digital strategy is online advertising. Platforms like Google Ads, Facebook Ads, or LinkedIn Ads allow you to segment your advertising campaigns with incredible precision, choosing who to show your ads to based on their geographic location, interests, behaviors, and many other factors. This is especially useful when you expand into new markets, as you can target specific audiences in the countries where you want to sell without wasting budget on people who aren't interested in your product or service. Plus, you can run A/B tests with different ads to see which messages and approaches work best in each market, thus optimizing your advertising investment.

Another important digital strategy for international trade is the use of e-commerce. Platforms such as Amazon, Alibaba, eBay or Shopify have greatly facilitated the process of selling products online to customers around the world. Through these platforms, you can not only reach a global audience, but you can also benefit from their logistics infrastructures and payment systems, allowing you to offer international shipping and handle different currencies efficiently. If you decide to use an e-commerce platform, it is important to ensure that your products are well presented, with clear and attractive descriptions, high-quality images and prices adapted to the local currency. In addition, it is essential to take into account the return and customer service policies for each market, as these factors also vary by region.

Search engine optimization (SEO) is another crucial component of any digital strategy for international trade. Ensuring that your website and content appear in search results in your target markets is essential to attracting organic traffic. This requires a market-specific approach, as search engines can vary from country to country. For example, while Google is the dominant search engine in most countries, in China the main search engine is Baidu, and in Russia it is Yandex. Tailoring your SEO strategy to these specific search engines is vital to gaining visibility in those markets.

Email marketing can also be a valuable tool in your international digital strategy. Although social media has gained popularity, email remains one of the most effective channels for communicating with customers in a direct and personalized way. You can use email marketing to send promotions, product news, or exclusive content to your international subscribers. However, it is essential to ensure that you comply with privacy and data protection laws in each country, such as the General Data Protection Regulation (GDPR) in Europe, which sets strict rules on how companies can collect and use consumer data.

Another key aspect to consider in your digital strategy for international trade is the online customer experience. Consumers in different countries have different expectations about what their online shopping experience should be like. For example, in some markets, customers expect local payment options, such as AliPay in China or iDEAL in the Netherlands. It's also important to consider expectations about shipping times and costs. While in some markets consumers are willing to wait longer for their products if shipping is free, in other markets, fast delivery times are a priority. Offering flexible, market-specific payment and shipping options will improve customer satisfaction and increase your chances of success.

Finally, data analysis is essential in any digital strategy for international trade. When selling in different countries, it is important to track and analyze data from your marketing campaigns, your web traffic, and your sales to identify which strategies are working best in each market.

Digital analytics tools, such as Google Analytics, can provide you with detailed insights into user behavior on your website, such as the pages they visit, the time they spend on the site, and conversion rates. Using this data to continually adjust and improve your digital strategy will allow you to optimize your efforts and get better results over time.

In short, digital strategies are essential for success in international trade. From having a strong, market-specific online presence to utilizing social media, online advertising, and e-commerce, all of these tools allow you to connect with customers around the world efficiently and effectively. Additionally, search engine optimization, email marketing, and online customer experience are key components to improving visibility and sales in international markets. And of course, don't forget the importance of analyzing data to adjust and improve your strategy over time. With a well-planned and executed digital strategy, you can expand your business globally and take advantage of the opportunities offered by international trade in the digital age.

Lucie Dupont

Logistics and International Supply Chain

Logistics and international supply chain are essential aspects for any company that wants to expand its business into other countries. As companies grow and begin selling in international markets, managing logistics efficiently becomes an even greater challenge. It is not just about moving products from one place to another; it involves coordinating a complex network of suppliers, carriers, warehouses and distributors to make sure that products arrive at the right destination, at the right time and at the lowest possible costs. In a global environment, where distances are greater and regulations vary between countries, logistics can be the difference between success and failure.

The supply chain is the entire process from the procurement of raw materials to the final delivery of the product to the customer. In an international context, the supply chain is complicated by geographical distances, differences in infrastructure, customs regulations and languages. Therefore, to operate globally, it is crucial to have a well-structured logistics system that can handle these challenges efficiently. This involves carefully planning how products will move, from the place where they are manufactured to the point of sale, taking into account the means of transport, transit times and costs.

One of the first steps in international logistics is choosing the most suitable means of transport for your products. The main options include air, sea or land transport, and each has its advantages and disadvantages. Air transport is fast, which is ideal for products that need to be delivered in a short time or those that are perishable, but it is much more expensive than other options. Sea transport, on the other hand, is cheaper and can move large volumes of products, but it is much slower. This is the most common method for non-perishable goods and large loads. Land transport is often a complementary option, used to distribute products within a country or between neighboring countries. Choosing the right transport method depends on the characteristics of the product, the market you are targeting, and the costs you are willing to assume.

In addition to choosing your shipping method, it's crucial to understand the customs and tariff regulations of the countries you want to ship your products to. Each country has its own laws and regulations regarding what products can be imported and under what conditions. Some products may require special licenses or meet specific standards before being accepted into a market. For example, food products, electronic devices, and pharmaceuticals are often subject to rigorous controls. Additionally, each country charges duties and taxes on the import of goods, and these costs can vary considerably depending on the type of product and the country of origin. It's critical to have a good team or business partners to help you navigate these regulations to avoid customs issues, delays, or even confiscation of your products.

Inventory management is another critical aspect of international logistics. Keeping enough products in stock to meet demand is important, but having too much inventory can increase storage costs and lead to waste, especially if the products are perishable or have a limited shelf life. In an international context, this is complicated by longer shipping times and the need to coordinate production and distribution across multiple countries. A common strategy is to have multiple distribution centers in different geographic regions to reduce lead times and optimize storage. This allows products to reach customers more quickly, reducing transportation costs and improving operational efficiency.

Technology plays a critical role in international supply chain management. Tools such as supply chain management (SCM) software allow companies to track and manage every step of the process, from ordering raw materials to final delivery of the product. These tools provide real-time visibility, which is vital for identifying potential problems before they become major issues. For example, if a shipment is delayed due to issues at customs, the software can alert logistics managers, who can take steps to mitigate the impact of the delay. In addition, technology also helps optimize transportation routes, improve warehousing efficiency, and better manage inventories, resulting in a more agile and efficient supply chain.

Another important aspect of international logistics is handling returns or reverse logistics. Not every product you ship will arrive in good condition or be accepted by customers. In some cases, products may be damaged during transport, or the customer may decide they no longer need them. In these cases, it is critical to have a plan in place to handle returns efficiently and cost-effectively. This may include having return centres in major market areas or establishing agreements with local carriers to facilitate the process of returning products. Reverse logistics is also important for recycling and waste management, which is increasingly relevant in a world where sustainability is a growing concern.

Sustainability, in fact, is gaining importance in international logistics. As consumers become more aware of the environmental impact of their purchases, companies must also adapt to reduce their carbon footprint and minimize the negative impact of their operations. This includes adopting greener transportation practices, such as using electric vehicles or cleaner fuels, and optimizing shipping routes to reduce carbon emissions. It also involves working with suppliers who share a focus on sustainability, using recyclable packaging and reducing waste in production and distribution.

Choosing your logistics partner is also crucial. In most cases, working with a third-party logistics company that has experience in international trade can greatly simplify the process. Not only do these partners have the right infrastructure and staff to handle large and complex shipments, but they are also typically experienced in customs regulations and the paperwork required to move products across borders. Choosing a reliable logistics partner will allow you to focus on other aspects of your business while they handle the details of shipping and delivery. However, it is important to select these partners carefully, as their efficiency and reliability will have a direct impact on customer experience.

Tracking and communicating with customers is also vital in international logistics. As products travel long distances, customers can become anxious about when they will receive their purchase. Providing real-time updates on the status of the shipment is a great way to keep customers informed and improve their experience. This can include using tracking codes, email or text message notifications, and offering access to an online portal where customers can view the progress of their order. Constant communication and transparency are essential to building trust and ensuring that customers are satisfied with the delivery process.

Finally, planning is key to successful international logistics. Every country has its own seasonal demand peaks, influenced by holidays, weather conditions, and other factors. For example, during the Chinese New Year, many factories in China close for an extended period, which can cause significant delays if not planned properly. Similarly, holiday seasons in Europe or North America can impact transportation capacity due to increased demand. Having a solid plan that considers these factors will allow you to avoid supply chain disruptions and ensure your products arrive on time.

In short, logistics and international supply chain are essential components for any business looking to expand globally. From choosing the right transportation to inventory management, customs regulations, and sustainability, each step in the process requires careful planning and the ability to adapt to the unique challenges presented by international trade. With the help of technology, reliable logistics partners, and a well-thought-out strategy, companies can overcome these challenges and take advantage of the opportunities offered by global trade to grow their business.

Lucie Dupont

Legal and Regulatory Compliance in International Sales

Legal and regulatory compliance is one of the most critical aspects to consider when a company decides to sell its products or services internationally. Laws and regulations can vary significantly from country to country, and making sure you comply with all of them is essential to avoid legal issues, penalties, fines, or even being banned from selling in certain markets. Although it may seem like a complex challenge, understanding and adapting to these regulations is critical to successful international sales. It is more than just a hurdle to overcome, it is an opportunity to build trust and credibility in foreign markets.

Every country has its own legal framework that regulates trade, and it's important to know your local laws in order to operate effectively. These laws can range from product regulations to tax laws, consumer protection laws, and data privacy laws. To start with, one of the main things to consider is regulatory compliance for the products you plan to sell. Some countries require products to go through a series of quality checks, safety tests, or meet certain standards before they can be marketed. For example, in the European Union, many products must bear the CE mark, which certifies that the product meets health, safety, and environmental requirements. If your product does not comply with these regulations, it cannot be legally sold in that market.

Another critical aspect of legal compliance is understanding the labeling and packaging laws in each country. Some markets have specific requirements regarding how information must be presented on products, what type of information must be included on labels, and what language it must be in. For example, in Canada, product labels must be in English and French, while in European Union countries, labels must be in the official language of each country. Additionally, certain products, such as food, cosmetics, or medicines, may be subject to stricter regulations that require detailed information about ingredients, directions for use, warnings, or allergens. Complying with these requirements is not only necessary to avoid legal problems, but it also helps to gain consumer trust.

Tax laws are another crucial aspect of legal compliance in international sales. Each country has its own tax laws that regulate the taxes you must pay for the sale of products or services in its territory. This can include import taxes, tariffs, and value-added tax (VAT) or sales taxes. Tariffs are fees charged for the import of goods into a country, and can vary depending on the type of product and its country of origin. Additionally, many countries require foreign companies to register a local entity or work with a tax representative to handle tax payments. Failing to comply with these tax obligations can have serious consequences, such as fines, shipment blocks, or the loss of the right to operate in that market. Therefore, it is critical to work with international tax experts or specialized accountants to ensure that you are complying with all tax regulations.

One of the most important issues in international trade today is the protection of personal data. In many countries, such as in the European Union with the General Data Protection Regulation (GDPR), there are strict laws that regulate how companies can collect, store, and use consumers' personal data. These laws seek to protect individuals' privacy and ensure that companies handle their data ethically and securely. If your company collects personal information from customers, such as their names, email addresses, or payment details, you must ensure that you comply with local privacy regulations. This involves, among other things, obtaining explicit consent from users before collecting their data, providing them with the ability to access and delete their information, and ensuring that the data is protected from potential security breaches. Failure to comply with these regulations can result in severe penalties, which in some cases can reach multi-million-dollar fines.

In addition to privacy laws, you should also be aware of consumer protection laws. These laws vary from country to country and are designed to protect the rights of consumers and ensure that they receive safe, high-quality products. Some of these laws require you to offer warranties or product return periods, while others may require you to provide customer service in the local language. Understanding and complying with these regulations is essential to ensure that your international customers have a positive shopping experience and to avoid legal issues.

Additionally, offering strong customer service that meets local expectations and regulations can help you differentiate yourself from the competition and gain consumer trust.

Compliance with international trade regulations can also involve issues related to intellectual property rights. If your company makes or sells innovative products, it is important to protect your intellectual property rights, such as patents, trademarks, or copyrights, in each country where you operate. Intellectual property laws vary from country to country, and in some markets it may be easier or more difficult to register and enforce your rights. Protecting your intellectual property rights is essential to prevent other companies from copying or imitating your products without your permission, which could harm your business. In addition, you also need to make sure that you do not infringe on the intellectual property rights of other companies in the international markets where you sell, as this could lead to lawsuits and legal problems.

In some international markets, there are also specific trade regulations, such as export restrictions or economic sanctions, that may affect your ability to do business in certain countries. For example, some countries may be subject to economic sanctions imposed by international bodies or foreign governments, meaning that doing business with them is prohibited or limited. It is essential to be aware of these regulations and ensure that your company does not violate any of them. This may involve doing prior research on the countries you plan to do business with and ensuring that they are not subject to trade sanctions or restrictions.

Finally, one of the best ways to ensure that you are complying with all international laws and regulations is to work with international trade lawyers. These professionals can help you navigate the legal complexities of foreign markets and ensure that your company is complying with all regulations. They can also help you draft international contracts, manage trade disputes, and ensure that you are adequately protecting your rights in the markets where you operate.

In short, legal and regulatory compliance in international sales is a critical aspect for any company looking to expand globally. From complying with product, label, and packaging regulations to navigating tax and data privacy laws, each step is essential to ensure your business operates safely and efficiently in foreign markets. While it may seem complicated, complying with these regulations not only prevents legal issues, but also strengthens the trust of consumers and business partners around the world. With the right advice and careful planning, you can ensure your business complies with all the regulations necessary to thrive in the global marketplace.

Lucie Dupont

International Taxes and Tariffs

International taxes and tariffs are an essential part of global trade, and any company that wants to sell overseas needs to understand how they work. These concepts may seem complicated, but they are simply tools that governments use to regulate the flow of goods between countries and collect revenue. If you're considering expanding your business internationally, it's crucial that you understand how international taxes and tariffs will affect your costs, your profit margins, and the competitiveness of your products in the global marketplace.

International taxes are, in essence, the tax obligations that a business has when it sells goods or services in another country. These taxes can take a variety of forms, such as value-added tax (VAT) or sales tax. Most countries impose a VAT or sales tax on imported goods, and this tax can vary widely by nation. For example, in some European countries, VAT can be as high as 20%, while in other countries it can be much lower. It's important to note that this tax is typically paid by the end consumer, but your business will be responsible for collecting it and remitting it to the tax authorities in the country you're selling in.

VAT is not the only type of tax you need to consider. In some countries, excise taxes may also apply to certain products, such as tobacco, alcohol, or luxury goods. These additional taxes can increase the final price of your products and affect their competitiveness in that market. In addition, some countries may require your company to register with their local tax system in order to legally operate and pay these taxes. This process can be complicated and vary greatly between countries, so it is advisable to have the support of tax advisors or accountants specialized in international trade.

Tariffs, on the other hand, are fees that governments charge for the importation of goods into their country. Tariffs are one of the main ways that governments protect their local economies and industries. When a tariff is imposed on an imported product, its final price increases, making it more expensive for local consumers compared to products made in the country. Tariffs vary depending on the type of product, its value, the country of origin, and the trade policies of the country imposing them. Some countries have very low tariffs or even free trade agreements with certain trading partners, meaning that some products can enter without paying tariffs or with reduced rates.

Understanding how tariffs work is crucial for any company that plans to export products. Tariffs can have a significant impact on the final price of your products and therefore on their competitiveness. For example, if you sell a product that is already expensive to manufacture, a high tariff could make it too expensive for consumers in a foreign market. Conversely, if you sell a product with a low manufacturing cost, you may be able to absorb some of the tariff and still be competitive. In any case, knowing in advance what tariffs apply to your products will help you better plan your pricing strategy in international markets.

One way to reduce tariffs or prevent their impact on your business is to take advantage of free trade agreements. Many countries have trade agreements with other nations that allow certain products to be traded with reduced or no tariffs. For example, the United States-Mexico-Canada Agreement (USMCA) allows many products to be traded between these three countries without tariffs. These agreements can be an excellent opportunity for companies looking to expand into new markets, as they remove one of the main obstacles to international trade: the cost of tariffs. However, to take advantage of these agreements, it is important to make sure that your products meet specific origin requirements, which means that they must have been manufactured for the most part in the countries that are part of the agreement.

Another important aspect to consider in relation to tariffs is the concept of customs value. This value refers to the price of the goods at the time they cross the border and is used to calculate tariffs. Typically, the customs value includes the cost of the goods as well as the cost of transport and insurance to the point of entry into the destination country. However, some countries may also include other costs, such as packaging costs or the cost of intellectual property rights, in the customs value. It is essential to ensure that the customs value is correctly declared to avoid problems with customs authorities and possible fines or penalties.

In addition to tariffs, businesses must also consider other trade barriers, such as import quotas. Quotas are restrictions that governments place on how much of a product can be imported in a given period. Once the quota has been reached, either no more goods of that type are allowed to be imported, or much higher additional tariffs are imposed on additional imports. This can be a challenge for businesses that rely on exporting large volumes of products to certain markets, as quotas can limit their ability to sell. To avoid problems with quotas, it is essential to carefully research and plan for entering new markets.

Compliance with tax and customs regulations is not only important to avoid legal penalties, but it can also have a significant impact on the logistics of your business. Customs delays are common when documents are not in order or when products do not comply with the regulations of the destination country. These delays not only increase storage and transportation costs, but can also cause problems with customers who expect to receive their products on time.

That's why it's essential to work with logistics and customs experts to help ensure that the entire import process goes smoothly. Additionally, it's important to stay on top of changes in trade policies, as governments may change tariffs and customs regulations in response to changes in the global economy or trade tensions with other countries.

An effective strategy for managing international taxes and tariffs is to engage in global tax planning. This involves analyzing the different tax and tariff regimes in the markets in which you want to operate and finding ways to optimize your tax structure. For example, some companies establish subsidiaries in countries with favorable tax regimes to reduce their overall tax burden. Other companies may take advantage of free trade zones, which are geographic areas where products can be imported, stored, and in some cases, processed without being subject to tariffs until they leave the free trade zone. These strategies require careful planning and, in many cases, the assistance of tax and legal advisors who specialize in international trade.

It's also important to keep in mind that international taxes and tariffs aren't static. They can change over time in response to economic, political, or social factors. For example, in recent years, we've seen an increase in trade tensions between some of the world's major economies, leading to the imposition of new tariffs and trade barriers. These changes can have a significant impact on your business if you're not prepared to adapt. That's why it's essential to stay on top of international trade news and trends and be flexible enough to adjust your strategy as needed.

In short, international taxes and tariffs are fundamental components of global trade. Understanding how they work and how they affect your business is essential to successfully planning your expansion into international markets. From VAT to tariffs, trade barriers and customs regulations, every aspect of international trade has an impact on your costs and the competitiveness of your products. With good planning, expert support, and a solid strategy, you can navigate these complexities and take advantage of the opportunities offered by global trade to successfully grow your business.

Lucie Dupont

Payment Methods and Currency Management in International Markets

When a company decides to sell its products or services in international markets, one of the most important aspects to consider is how it will receive payments and how it will handle foreign currencies. Unlike local sales, where payments are usually direct and in the same currency, international sales involve greater complexity due to the different payment methods available and currency fluctuations. Choosing the right payment methods and effectively managing foreign currencies can make a big difference in the financial success of your business abroad.

One of the first challenges businesses face when selling internationally is deciding which payment methods to offer their customers. Depending on the country, payment culture and consumer preferences can vary greatly. For example, in some European countries, the use of bank transfers is very common, while in Latin America, payment in installments or through e-wallets may be preferred. In Asia, payment through mobile apps is a growing trend. Offering payment methods that best suit each market is crucial to facilitate transactions and increase sales. Therefore, it is essential to research the most popular payment options in each country where you plan to sell and make sure your business can accept those methods.

Common forms of international payment include credit cards, bank transfers, payments through digital platforms such as PayPal or Stripe, and letters of credit. Credit cards are a popular option globally, and most businesses accept them for their convenience and speed. However, it is important to remember that fees associated with card processing can vary by country and payment service provider. Bank transfers, while a secure way to receive payments, often take longer to complete and may incur additional fees for both the buyer and the seller.

Another common method of payment in international trade is the letter of credit. This is a financial agreement in which a bank acts as an intermediary, ensuring that the seller receives payment only if certain conditions are met, such as delivery of the goods within a certain time frame or presentation of specific documents. Letters of credit are especially useful when doing business with new customers or in markets where trade laws are not as clear. They offer an extra layer of security for both the buyer and the seller, as they reduce the risk of non-payment. However, they can be costly and require more complex bureaucratic handling, which may not be suitable for all businesses or transactions.

In addition to choosing the right payment methods, another critical aspect of international sales is currency management. When selling in multiple countries, your customers are likely to pay in different currencies, which means you'll need to convert those currencies to your local currency in order to use them. The value of currencies constantly fluctuates due to various economic, political, and social factors, which can have a direct impact on your revenue and profits. If you don't manage currency risk properly, you could lose a significant portion of your profits simply due to a drop in the value of a foreign currency.

One of the first decisions you need to make is what currency you're going to price your products in. Some businesses choose to offer prices in the local currency of each country, which makes it easier for customers to purchase and offers greater transparency. However, this also means that your business will have to deal with the fluctuation of multiple currencies, which can increase financial risk. Another option is to set prices in a stable international currency, such as the US dollar or the euro. This reduces currency risk for your business, but can make your products less attractive to customers in countries with weaker currencies, as their purchasing power could be affected.

To better manage the risk of currency fluctuations, many businesses use financial instruments such as futures contracts or currency hedges. These instruments allow you to lock in the exchange rate at a future date, protecting you against adverse currency fluctuations. For example, if you know you will be paid in euros in three months, but you fear that the value of the euro may fall in that time, you can use a futures contract to ensure that you will receive a favorable exchange rate no matter what happens in the market. While these types of financial instruments may seem complicated, working with specialized financial advisors or banks can help you implement these strategies effectively.

Another important aspect of currency handling is the cost of currency conversion. When converting payments from one currency to another, banks and payment platforms often charge fees for the service, as well as applying an exchange rate that may not be as favorable as the one listed on the market. These costs can significantly reduce your profit margins, especially if you operate in multiple countries. That's why it's essential to work with banks or payment service providers that offer competitive fees and fair exchange rates. You may also want to consider opening bank accounts in the major currencies you operate in to avoid the need to frequently convert currencies and thus reduce costs.

An increasingly popular option for handling international payments and currencies is the use of digital payment platforms that allow for quick currency conversions with lower fees than traditional banks. Services like PayPal, Stripe, or Wise offer payment solutions that allow businesses to accept payments in multiple currencies and automatically convert them to the preferred currency. These platforms also often offer detailed reporting on transactions, making accounting and financial planning easier. Plus, their simplicity and global reach make them an attractive option for small and medium-sized businesses that don't have the resources to manage complex international banking operations.

It's also important to consider the tax implications of dealing with foreign currencies. In some countries, profits from exchange rate differences may be subject to tax, so it's crucial to work with an accountant or tax advisor who understands the tax laws of both your country and the markets where you operate. Additionally, international transactions may require you to file additional reports or meet specific requirements related to handling foreign currencies. Failure to comply with these requirements could result in penalties or audits that could negatively impact your business.

Ultimately, good payment and currency management in international markets is critical to ensuring your business remains profitable. It's not just about choosing the most appropriate payment methods, but also effectively managing currency risk, reducing currency conversion costs, and complying with tax regulations. By doing so, you can ensure your business is competitive and efficient in the global marketplace, allowing you to grow and thrive in new regions. As with any aspect of international trade, having expert support and using the right tools will help you navigate these complexities and make the most of the opportunities that global markets offer.

Lucie Dupont

Contracts and Negotiation in International Sales

When it comes to international sales, one of the most important aspects to master is contract drafting and negotiation. Unlike domestic sales, where laws and business practices are typically clear and uniform, in international sales you are faced with a more complex landscape. Differences in legal systems, cultural barriers, languages, and regulations can make creating a solid contract and negotiating more challenging processes. However, mastering these elements is crucial to protecting your business, ensuring transactions go smoothly, and avoiding misunderstandings that can have costly consequences.

The sales contract is the legal document that sets out the terms and conditions of a transaction. In an international contract, it is vital that all aspects of the agreement are clearly defined, as the laws governing trade can vary significantly from one country to another. A good international sales contract should cover key points such as the detailed description of the goods or services, the price, the method of payment, the delivery time, the conditions of transport and any guarantees or liabilities. Unlike a simple verbal agreement, the contract is the legal basis that will protect you in case any problems or conflicts arise with the buyer.

One of the first things to consider when drafting an international contract is deciding which law will apply to the agreement. That is, in which country will any potential disputes be resolved? This is especially important because one country's business laws can be very different from another's. In some cases, companies choose to use a neutral jurisdiction, such as the International Chamber of Commerce (ICC) international law, which sets widely accepted global standards. This way, both parties feel more comfortable, knowing that the contract will be governed by a set of known and fair rules. If you don't clearly define the applicable law, you could find yourself in a tricky situation, trying to resolve a dispute in a country with a legal system you're not familiar with.

Another key aspect of international contracts is the language in which they are drafted. While it is common to use English as the international language of business, not all countries and businesspeople have the same level of proficiency in this language. To avoid misunderstandings or misinterpretations, it is advisable that the contract be drafted in the languages of both parties or, at least, that an official translation be included. Although this may entail additional costs, having a contract that is clear and understandable to both parties is essential to avoid disputes that may arise due to language differences.

Negotiation in international sales is an art that requires not only business skills, but also a deep understanding of the cultures and customs of the countries you are negotiating with. In many cases, what is acceptable and effective in a negotiation in one country may not be so in another. For example, in some Asian countries, such as Japan or China, negotiation is a slow process based on building long-term relationships of trust. Interrupting the other party or being too direct can be interpreted as disrespectful. In contrast, in Western countries, such as the United States or Germany, negotiations tend to be faster and more direct, focusing on facts and efficiency. Adapting your negotiation style to local customs is crucial to successfully closing deals.

It is important to keep an open mind and be willing to compromise during international negotiations. Cultural differences can lead to misunderstandings or disagreements, but if you approach negotiations with a collaborative, rather than competitive, attitude, you are more likely to find solutions that benefit both parties. At the same time, it is essential to know your limits and not give in on those points that are vital to the success of your business. Finding the balance between flexibility and firmness is a key skill in any negotiation, but it is even more important in an international context, where cultural and language differences can complicate things.

During the negotiation, it is also important to be prepared to address issues related to payment terms, delivery times, and responsibilities in case something goes wrong. For example, delivery conditions can be a source of disagreement if they are not clearly addressed from the beginning. In international trade, incoterms, which are international rules that define the responsibilities of the buyer and seller regarding the transport and delivery of products, play a key role. Making sure that both parties agree on the incoterms and who will be responsible for the costs and risks during transport is essential to avoid problems down the road.

Another aspect to consider when negotiating international contracts is the question of warranties and liability. While in some jurisdictions it is common for the seller to offer guarantees on the quality of the product or the performance of the service, in other markets this may not be an expectation. It is essential that these types of details are discussed and clearly reflected in the contract. If the product has some type of guarantee, it is important to specify the conditions and term of the guarantee, as well as the steps that the buyer must follow in case he needs to claim it. Clearly defining these aspects will help to avoid misunderstandings and protect both the seller and the buyer.

As for dispute resolution methods, it is advisable for international contracts to include an arbitration clause. Arbitration is a way of resolving disputes outside of court, through a neutral arbitrator who issues a decision that is binding on both parties. This option is often preferred in international trade because it is faster, less expensive, and more flexible than traditional court procedures. In addition, arbitration allows the parties to choose an arbitrator with experience in the specific sector of the dispute, ensuring that the final decision is fair and well-informed. Including an arbitration clause in the contract also helps to give both parties peace of mind, as they know that, should a dispute arise, they will be able to resolve it quickly and effectively.

In addition to legal and business aspects, it's also important to consider logistics when negotiating international contracts. Differences in time zones, geographic distance, and language barriers can make coordination between parties more difficult. For example, if you're negotiating with a company in Asia while your company is in Europe or America, time differences are likely to make communication slower and require more planning. Ensuring that delivery times, communication expectations, and follow-up processes are clearly defined in the contract will help you overcome these challenges and ensure that everything runs smoothly.

Finally, one of the most important factors to consider when negotiating and drafting international contracts is trust. Although international sales may involve greater risks due to distance and legal differences, building a strong relationship based on mutual trust is essential for long-term success. While the contract is the legal tool that protects you, trust and good communication with your client or business partner are critical to ensuring that both parties honor their commitments and resolve any issues constructively. Showing respect for local customs, being transparent in communication, and keeping your promises are some of the ways you can foster a relationship of trust, which in turn will make future negotiations smoother and more successful.

In short, negotiating and creating contracts in international sales are complex processes that require careful planning and attention to detail. From choosing the applicable law to defining payment terms and delivery responsibilities, every aspect of the contract must be carefully considered to avoid misunderstandings and protect the interests of your business. Additionally, adapting to cultural differences in negotiations and building relationships of trust are key elements to ensuring long-term success in international trade. By approaching these challenges with an open and flexible attitude, you will be better prepared to take advantage of the opportunities offered by global markets and successfully grow your business.

Pricing Strategies for International Markets

Determining an effective pricing strategy for international markets is one of the most crucial steps when you decide to expand your business across borders. Pricing appropriately not only ensures that you are competitive, but also allows you to cover your costs and maximize your profits. However, setting prices in international markets is much more complicated than simply converting your local market prices to foreign currency. There are a number of additional factors that need to be taken into account, such as local costs, consumer expectations, competitors, and government policies. That's why designing a smart and well-informed pricing strategy is key to success in global trade.

The first step in establishing an international pricing strategy is to assess the additional costs involved in selling in foreign markets. When selling in another country, you must consider not only production costs, but also expenses related to transportation, customs, tariffs, local taxes, and in some cases, currency conversion costs. All of these elements can significantly increase the final price of your product. If you do not take these costs into account, you could set a price that is too low to cover your expenses or, on the contrary, a price so high that you are put out of business. It is essential to conduct a detailed analysis of all the costs involved in selling internationally to ensure that your prices are profitable and competitive.

In addition to costs, it is also important to understand consumer expectations in different markets. The value that customers perceive in a product can vary greatly from one country to another. What may be considered a premium product in your local market may be seen as a commodity in another market, or vice versa. For example, consumers in some countries are willing to pay more for imported products due to the perception of higher quality or exclusivity. In other markets, however, consumers might be more price-sensitive and prefer cheaper local alternatives. Understanding how they perceive your product and what value they place on it is essential to effectively adjusting your prices.

Another key variable in international pricing strategy is competition. Before setting a price, you should research how your competitors are positioned in the market you are targeting. If your product is similar to those already on the market, your price should be competitive, either lower or with a clear added value that justifies a higher price. However, if your product offers unique features or is innovative, you might have the opportunity to charge a premium price. In any case, competitor analysis is essential to ensure that you are not setting a price that will alienate customers or, on the contrary, one that will not allow you to make adequate profits.

One of the most common strategies in international pricing is the tiered pricing strategy, also known as "localized pricing." This means adjusting your product prices based on the local market. Prices can vary from country to country due to differences in costs, competition, and consumer purchasing power. For example, you might sell your product at a higher price in a country with a high standard of living and a luxury market, while in another country with lower purchasing power, the price should be lower to attract customers. While this strategy can increase sales in specific local markets, it can also lead to complications if consumers find out they are paying more than in other countries. In the age of globalization and access to information, tiered pricing must be managed carefully so as not to affect your brand reputation.

Another option for setting international prices is the standardized pricing strategy, which involves setting a fixed price in all markets, regardless of local costs or market conditions. This approach can simplify price management and give a sense of fairness among consumers in different countries. However, it may not be suitable in markets with large differences in costs or purchasing power. For example, if you set a price too high in a country with a weaker economy, you could lose sales. At the same time, setting a price too low in a high-standard-of-living market could cause your product to be perceived as low quality. The key with this strategy is to find a balance that allows you to be competitive in all markets without compromising your profit margins.

Another strategy that can be useful in international markets is penetration pricing. This involves setting a low initial price to quickly enter a new market, attract customers, and gain market share. Once you establish yourself and build a solid customer base, you can gradually increase prices. This strategy can be effective when your goal is to gain visibility and presence in a new market, especially if you face strong competition. However, you must be careful not to set prices so low that they affect the perception of the quality of your product or harm your profit margins in the long run.

On the other hand, if your product has a unique feature or is perceived as high quality, you may opt for a premium pricing strategy. This involves setting a higher price than your competitors, which gives the impression that your product is exclusive or luxury. This strategy can be particularly effective in markets where consumers associate high price with quality or prestige. However, you need to make sure that your product actually offers superior value and is aligned with consumer expectations. A premium price without a clear justification can cause customers to look for cheaper alternatives.

An additional factor to consider when setting international prices is currency fluctuations. Exchange rates can vary significantly over short periods of time, affecting the actual price customers will pay and the profits you will receive. To mitigate the risk of currency fluctuations, some companies choose to set prices in a stable currency, such as the US dollar or euro, regardless of the customer's local currency. Another option is to use financial hedging strategies to protect against exchange rate fluctuations. Whichever option you choose, it's important to consider the impact of currencies on your prices and be prepared to adjust them if necessary.

In addition to all these considerations, it is also crucial to take into account government policies and local market regulations that may affect your pricing. In some countries, governments impose price controls on certain products, especially in essential sectors such as food or medicine. There may also be restrictions on how much you can increase prices or additional taxes that affect the final cost of your product. Before launching your product in a new market, it is important to research all local regulations that may influence your pricing strategy to avoid legal or financial issues.

Finally, remember that pricing for international markets is not a static process. As market conditions change, competitors introduce new products, or local economies experience fluctuations, it may be necessary to adjust your prices to remain competitive. It's important to constantly monitor the factors that affect your prices and be willing to make adjustments when necessary. A well-informed, flexible pricing strategy will allow you to adapt to changing conditions and maximize your chances of success in international markets.

In short, designing a pricing strategy for international markets is a complex process that requires taking into account many factors, from local costs and competition to consumer expectations and currency fluctuations. There is no one-size-fits-all formula that works for every business, so it is essential that you do thorough research and consider all options before making a decision. Whether you opt for a differentiated, standardized, or penetration pricing strategy, the most important thing is that your strategy is consistent with your business goals and the characteristics of the markets in which you operate. With proper planning and a flexible attitude, you will be able to set prices that allow you to grow and prosper in the competitive world of international trade.

Lucie Dupont

Customer Service and Support in the Global Market

Customer service and support in the global marketplace are critical pieces to the success of any business looking to expand internationally. When you sell in multiple countries, you're not just competing for the best product or the most attractive price, you're also competing to offer the best customer experience. And in many cases, what truly sets a successful brand apart in global commerce is not so much what it sells, but how it treats its customers. In international markets, where cultural, language and expectation differences are more apparent, offering high-quality customer service can be what keeps customers choosing your brand again and again.

The first key aspect of global customer support is local language availability. You can't expect international customers to perfectly speak or understand the language in which you operate your business. That's why having trained staff who speak the local language or having a translation service can make a big difference. Customers feel more comfortable when they can express their questions or problems in their own language, and this increases trust in your brand. If you can't offer support in all languages, an alternative is to start with the most common languages among your international customers, such as English, Spanish, or French, and then expand to other languages as needed.

However, it's not just about translating words, but understanding the cultural differences that can influence how customer service is expected to be. For example, in some countries, customers value speed and efficiency above all else. In these cases, response time is critical, and the company that responds first to queries is likely to win more customers. In other countries, customers prefer a more personalized and personal approach, where long-term relationships and trust are prioritized. Knowing how to adapt your customer service style to local cultural expectations is crucial to offering a service that truly satisfies your customers in each region.

Another important aspect is the accessibility of customer support. When you sell globally, your customers can be anywhere in the world, which means they may have very different schedules than your customer support team. Imagine a customer in Japan trying to contact you, but they can only do so during their country's business hours, and it turns out that your support team is in a country with a completely different time zone. This kind of mismatch can lead to frustration and a poor customer experience. To avoid this, it's ideal to offer multiple customer support channels, such as email, live chat, or even chatbots, that are available 24 hours a day. This ensures that no matter the time difference, customers can get help when they need it.

It's also important to consider the platforms your international customers use. In some parts of the world, email is still the preferred means of contacting a business, while in other regions, messaging apps like WhatsApp or WeChat are much more popular. Adapting to the tools and platforms your customers regularly use can significantly improve the quality of your customer service. There's no point in offering a support channel that your customers don't use or find inconvenient. By choosing the right platforms for each market, you show that you understand and respect local preferences.

The quality of technical and after-sales support is also a decisive factor in international customer satisfaction. When customers have problems with a product or service, they want a fast and effective solution, no matter where they are. In some cases, this may mean having local service centers or a network of partners who can provide in-person support. In other cases, it may be enough to offer a helpline staffed by experts who speak the local language and are trained to solve technical problems. Either way, the important thing is that customers feel they can trust you to solve any problem they have with your product, no matter where they are in the world.

Another key aspect is the ability to manage customer expectations from the start. When you sell internationally, differences in delivery times, return policies, and warranties can vary significantly from country to country. It's important to be transparent with your customers about what they can expect in each of these aspects. For example, if shipping to a specific country takes longer than usual due to local regulations or geographic distances, it's important for customers to know this from the start. Likewise, if return policies or warranties are different in certain markets, this should also be made clear. Transparency not only prevents misunderstandings, but also increases trust in your brand.

Personalization also plays a big role in global customer service. In international trade, customers want to feel like they're not just another number on a buyer's list. Even though you're selling in different countries, it's important to find ways to personalize the customer experience so they feel valued and heard. This can be achieved through personalized messages, offers tailored to their preferences, or simply remembering details about their previous purchases. In some markets, personalization can be as simple as including a personalized greeting in their language, while in others, customers may expect a deeper level of attention to their needs.

Of course, it's also essential to continually measure and improve the quality of your customer service. In a global environment, where each market may have its own expectations and challenges, it's crucial to gather feedback from your customers in each country. This will allow you to identify areas where you can improve and adapt your processes to offer better service. Conducting satisfaction surveys, analysing common complaints and reviewing response times are some of the ways you can ensure your customer service is meeting the standards your international customers expect.

Finally, technology plays a key role in global customer service. Using tools like customer relationship management (CRM) systems allows you to keep a detailed record of all interactions with your customers, regardless of where they are located. These systems allow you to track queries, resolve issues faster, and deliver a consistent experience across all customer service channels. Additionally, AI tools like chatbots can help answer common questions instantly, improving customer experience and reducing the workload on your support team.

In conclusion, customer service in the global market is much more than solving problems. It is a powerful tool for building long-term relationships, building customer loyalty, and differentiating yourself from the competition. From offering support in the local language to adapting to cultural differences and managing customer expectations, every aspect of international customer service requires careful planning and a service-oriented attitude. By implementing solid strategies that address these challenges, you will not only improve your customers' experience, but you will also position yourself as a trustworthy company committed to their satisfaction, no matter where they are in the world.

Lucie Dupont

Building International Sales Teams

Building international sales teams is a crucial step for any company looking to expand globally. A well-structured sales team aligned with your business goals can make the difference between success and failure in international markets. However, building a team that works globally is not as simple as replicating the model you use in your home country. It requires planning, adaptation, and a clear strategy that takes into account cultural differences, local markets, and long-distance coordination.

The first step in building an international sales team is to make sure you have people who understand the local market. Selling in a foreign country isn't just about speaking the language – although that certainly helps – but about understanding how customers in that region think and act. This includes knowing their buying habits, their needs, and the barriers they may face when purchasing a product or service. That's why many companies choose to hire local staff – people who not only speak the language, but are also immersed in the culture and environment of that market. These people can offer insight that an outsider, no matter how skilled, simply couldn't have.

In addition to hiring local talent, it is critical for international sales teams to work towards a common goal. Despite geographical and cultural differences, all members of a global sales team must be aligned with the company's vision and goals. This involves having a clear and well-defined sales strategy that is tailored to different markets, but also maintains global consistency. To achieve this, it is important for companies to invest time in training their teams, not only in sales techniques, but also in the company's culture and values. This will help ensure that, no matter where they are in the world, all salespeople consistently represent the brand.

Another challenge that arises when building international sales teams is communication. Distance and time differences can make coordination between team members difficult. That's why it's crucial to have technological tools that facilitate real-time communication, such as video calling platforms, instant messaging, and project management software. These tools allow teams to stay in touch and work collaboratively, no matter where they are. Additionally, it's important to establish clear communication channels and times when all team members can meet to discuss strategies, share experiences, and solve problems. Good communication is the foundation for the team to function as a cohesive unit.

However, communication is not just about technology – it also requires interpersonal skills. In an international sales team, members are likely to come from very different cultures, which means that the way they communicate and work can vary. Some cultures value hierarchy more and prefer formal, structured communication, while others are more open and favour direct, less formal communication. To manage these differences, team leaders must be sensitive to cultural particularities and ensure that everyone feels comfortable contributing and sharing ideas. Promoting a culture of mutual respect and collaboration is key to overcoming cultural barriers and achieving effective communication.

Another important aspect to consider when building an international sales team is motivation. Salespeople, like any other employee, need to feel valued and motivated to do their best. However, what motivates employees can vary from country to country. In some markets, financial incentives such as bonuses and commissions can be a strong motivator, while in others, employees value job security, growth opportunities, or public recognition more. It's important to understand what motivates your team in each region and tailor your compensation and motivation strategies accordingly. There is no one-size-fits-all approach that works in every market, so it's critical to be flexible and willing to adjust strategies for each context.

Furthermore, it is essential to invest in ongoing training for your international sales team. The world of global trade is constantly changing, with new trends, technologies and skills emerging all the time. Training your team not only in the latest sales techniques, but also in the culture of the country where they operate, the particularities of the local market and the product they offer is an investment that will translate into better results. Training also offers the opportunity to align teams with the company's global objectives and to reinforce the importance of a coherent sales strategy across all markets.

Once you've built your international sales team, it's important to measure performance on an ongoing basis. This will allow you to identify which strategies are working and which ones need adjustment. When working with teams in different countries, it's crucial to have clear metrics that allow you to compare performance across markets. However, you need to be careful not to fall into the trap of directly comparing results across very different regions. Each market has its own challenges and opportunities, so it's important to contextualize results and adjust expectations based on the particularities of each region.

Finally, leading an international sales team requires effective and flexible management. It is not enough to simply give instructions and hope that everything works. Leaders must be available to support their teams, solve problems and adapt to changes that may arise in each market. In addition, it is essential that leaders promote an inclusive work culture, where all team members feel valued and have the opportunity to contribute their ideas and knowledge. By leading with empathy and adaptability, international sales managers can bring out the best in their teams and create a culture of collaboration and success on a global level.

In short, building international sales teams is a complex process that requires planning, effective communication, cultural sensitivity, and a healthy dose of flexibility. By hiring local talent, aligning them with the company's global goals, fostering open communication, and training them on an ongoing basis, you can build a sales team that not only understands local markets but is also able to work in harmony with the rest of the organization. With a clear strategy and effective management, international sales teams can become the backbone of your company's global growth.

Constant Innovation and Adaptation

Innovation and constant adaptation are critical to success in an ever-changing global business world. As companies expand into new international markets, they face an increasingly competitive environment, where customer expectations are evolving rapidly and technologies are advancing at a dizzying pace. To survive and thrive in this environment, it is not enough to have a quality product or service. You need to always be one step ahead, anticipate changes and be willing to modify strategies and practices to adapt to new market realities.

Innovation, in its broadest sense, is not just about creating new and exciting products. In the context of international sales, it also means finding more efficient and effective ways of doing things. This could be improving production processes to reduce costs, optimising the supply chain to shorten lead times, or using new technologies to improve the customer experience. Innovation is always about looking for ways to do things better, faster or more efficiently – not just to keep up with the competition, but to outperform it.

However, innovation does not happen spontaneously. To foster a culture of innovation within a company, you need to create an environment that allows for it. This means that employees must feel comfortable proposing ideas, trying out new strategies and taking calculated risks. Companies that encourage their teams to think creatively and seek innovative solutions are the ones that tend to stand out in global markets. Often, the best ideas come from those who are in direct contact with customers or with the day-to-day operations, as they are the ones who best understand the real problems and opportunities for improvement.

Furthermore, it is crucial that innovation is geared towards customer needs. There is no point in developing a new technology or sales strategy if it does not somehow improve the customer experience. International markets can be very different from one another, so the expectations and needs of consumers in one country will not be the same as in another. Innovating also means adapting to these differences. Perhaps in one country you need to focus on improving delivery speed, while in another the most important thing is to offer customer service in the local language. The key is to listen to customers and understand what they really value in each market.

On the other hand, constant adaptation is just as important as innovation. The global market is in constant motion, and what worked yesterday may not be effective tomorrow. Trends change, competitors become stronger, and regulations may vary. Adapting quickly to these changes is essential to survive in the international business environment. Companies that remain rigid in their approaches or resist change risk being left behind. Those that are agile and flexible, on the other hand, have the ability to adjust their strategy in response to new market conditions and, consequently, have a greater chance of success.

A good example of adaptation is how companies have had to adjust to new digital technologies. In recent decades, global commerce has changed dramatically thanks to the internet, social media and e-commerce platforms. Companies that did not adopt these technologies in time or that did not adapt to the new way consumers shop and communicate lost ground to more agile competitors. Adapting to digitalization is not just a matter of being present online, but of taking advantage of all the tools and opportunities offered by the digital world to improve sales processes, marketing and customer relations.

Adaptation also involves staying abreast of changes in international rules and regulations. Governments in different countries may impose new laws or requirements that directly affect the way business is conducted. This may include changes in import and export policies, new tax rules, or stricter environmental regulations. Companies that succeed in international markets are those that closely monitor these changes and adjust their operations to comply with regulations without losing efficiency. Ignoring or underestimating the importance of these regulations can result in costly penalties or loss of access to a key market.

Leadership also plays a key role in fostering both innovation and adaptation. Business leaders must be proactive, willing to challenge the status quo and be early adopters of new ideas and technologies. They must also foster an environment in which change is not feared but seen as an opportunity for improvement. Leaders who inspire their teams to be innovative and remain flexible in the face of change are those who guide their companies to success in international markets.

Another key aspect of innovation and adaptation is the ability to learn from mistakes. Not every innovative initiative will succeed, and not every adaptation will be effective immediately. However, companies that have a growth mindset and see failures as opportunities to learn and improve are the ones that ultimately thrive. The key is to be agile enough to recognize when something isn't working and adjust strategy quickly to correct course. This requires humility and openness, but it is one of the best ways to ensure long-term success.

In today's globalized world, competition can come from any corner of the planet. This means that it is not enough to be good at what you do; you must be constantly looking for ways to do it better. Innovating and adapting are not only tools for growth, but for surviving in an environment that is increasingly unpredictable. Companies that stand out internationally are those that make innovation and constant adaptation an integral part of their business culture.

In short, innovation and constant adaptation are fundamental pillars for success in international trade. Innovation does not only mean creating new products or using advanced technology, but also always looking for ways to improve processes and adapt to changing customer needs. Adaptation, on the other hand, involves being flexible and responding quickly to changes in the market, trends, regulations and consumer expectations. By making innovation and adaptation a priority, companies can not only stay competitive, but also lead in the globalized and constantly changing world that defines international trade today.

www.ingramcontent.com/pod-product-compliance
Lightning Source LLC
Chambersburg PA
CBHW031430150726
47989CB00002B/889